OLD OCEAN CITY

MEMORIES OF OCEAN CITY

OLD OCEAN CITY

THE JOURNAL AND PHOTOGRAPHS OF ROBERT CRAIGHEAD WALKER, 1904–1916

C. John Sullivan

The Johns Hopkins University Press

Baltimore & London

© 2001 The Johns Hopkins University Press

All rights reserved. Published 2001

Printed in China

on acid-free paper

9 8 7 6 5 4 3 2 1

The Johns Hopkins University Press

2715 North Charles Street

Baltimore, Maryland 21218-4363

www.press.jhu.edu

Library of Congress Cataloging-in-Publication Data

Walker, Robert C. (Robert Craighead), 1894–1966.

Old Ocean City : the journal and photography of

Robert Craighead Walker, 1904–1916 /

[compiled by] C. John Sullivan.

p. cm.

ISBN 0-8018-6585-9 (alk. paper)

1. Ocean City (Md.)—History—20th century—
Pictorial works. 2. Ocean City (Md.)—Biography.
3. Ocean City (Md.)—Social life and customs—20th
century. 4. Walker, Robert C. (Robert Craighead),
1894–1966—Diaries. 5. Walker, Robert C. (Robert
Craighead), 1894–1966—Childhood and youth.
6. Walker family. I. Sullivan, C. John. II. Title.

F189.02 W35 2001

975.2'21—dc21   00-009629

A catalog record for this book is available

from the British Library.

To the family of

William G. Walker and

Nannie Letitia Walker

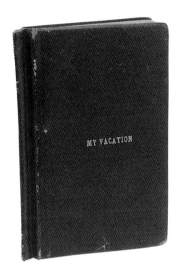

Contents

———

PREFACE

OR THOSE of us who love history, the memories of our youth become our own history. Growing up in Maryland, reared between the mountains and the ocean, was a blessing to me. I cannot imagine a life far from the water. My family's annual pilgrimage to Ocean City began in the late 1940s. My first recollection of that bright white beach and the sound and smell of the surf became ingrained in my memory and draws me back each year. Crossing the Sinepuxent Bay and having the smell of the ocean fill my head blinds my sight to the modern high rises and takes me back to the Ocean City of my youth.

Vacationers of today can only dream of what this seaside resort was like for those who visited in the early 1900s. The Walkers of Washington, D.C., were one such family.

The Walkers resided in Washington at 706 A Street, S.E., in a large brownstone. William G. Walker married Nannie Letitia Wheat in Washington in August 1892, and the couple honeymooned in Ocean City. Their family grew to include three children: the oldest, Robert Craighead Walker, born in 1894, and two daughters—Letitia, born in 1900, and Margaret, born in 1906. They returned to Ocean City together for summer vacations for many years.

THE WALKERS' RESIDENCE AT
706 A STREET, S.E., WASHINGTON, D.C.,
NOVEMBER 10, 1905

NANNIE LETITIA WHEAT WALKER, NOVEMBER 1893,
ONE YEAR AFTER HER MARRIAGE

When the Walker family visited Ocean City after the turn of the century, it was to enjoy summers filled with target practice on the beach, hunting the abundant waterfowl, fishing, boating, picnicking, and bathing in the ocean. By 1910 William Walker had built a summer cottage, which still stands at the corner of Baltimore Avenue and Seventh Street, and Ocean City became the family's summer home. He purchased the lot in 1908 from the Sinepuxent Beach Company of

ROBERT CRAIGHEAD WALKER,
NOVEMBER 9, 1901, AGE 7 YEARS,
3 MONTHS, 8 DAYS

WILLIAM G. WALKER, NOVEMBER 1893

xii

NANNIE LETITIA WALKER AND
WILLIAM G. WALKER WITH THEIR ELDEST
CHILD, ROBERT, AT OCEAN CITY,
MARYLAND, IN 1903

ROBERT C. WALKER WITH HIS
NEW RIFLE SURROUNDED BY FAMILY
AND FRIENDS, 1904

NANNIE AND HER DAUGHTER, LETITIA,
DRESSED FOR THE AFTERNOON;
OCEAN CITY, AUGUST 1, 1908

ROBERT AND LETITIA,
SEPTEMBER 1904

xiv

NANNIE AND MARGARET,
AUGUST 1910

EFFIE'S DAUGHTER AND A COMPANION,
ABOUT 1910

EFFIE WITH LETITIA WALKER
AT ROMARLETTA

MARGARET, NANNIE, AND LETITIA
ON THE PORCH OF ROMARLETTA
IN AUGUST 1910

Baltimore City and initially constructed a small hunting lodge on it. Walker named the cottage "Romarletta" in honor of his three children: "Ro" for Robert,
"Mar" for Margaret, and "Letta" for Letitia. Each
summer the Walkers traveled from Washington to
Ocean City by train and boat to set up housekeeping
at their cottage until it was once again time to close up
the cottage and return to the city.

DOROTHY VAN DER VEER
AND MARGARET WALKER,
AUGUST 1916

FROM THE PORCH OF ROMARLETTA
SEPTEMBER 8, 1914: "THINGS ARE NOT
ALWAYS WHAT THEY SEEM."

The following pages chronicle those long ago summers through the words and photographs of the Walker family. Avid photographers as well as sportsmen, the Walkers preserved their Ocean City summers in hundreds of photographs, some of which appear in this volume. The Walkers' son, Robert, also recorded the details of those days in a small leather-bound journal, titled *My Vacation*, in which he wrote almost daily from 1912 to 1916. Together, photographs and journal give us a unique glimpse into the summer experience of Ocean City's earliest vacationers. Yet, to an extent, this volume also represents the collective summer experiences of generations of Ocean City vacationers. The mode of travel to the seashore has changed, the town has grown, and shooting of shorebirds from the beaches is a distant memory; but vacationers still come to bathe in the surf, boat, fish, dine in favorite restaurants, and amuse themselves on the boardwalk in the evenings.

ACKNOWLEDGMENTS

MY LIFELONG friend Henry A.
Fleckenstein Jr. led me to an attic in
Berlin, Maryland, on one of those hot,
muggy days in the late summer of 1994.
It was there that we shared our first glimpse of a hand-
ful of amazing old photos of Ocean City, Maryland,
but it was an Ocean City far different than our memories could recall. The photos were the work of
William G. Walker, a dedicated photographer and
sportsman who taught his son, Robert Craighead
Walker, to view the world around him with the same
keen, artistic sensibility.

Robert's son, Donald V. Walker, the owner of that
sweltering attic and the caretaker of his family's photos, proved to be a generous and patient host through

numerous visits. His historical insights, along with those of his sister, Anne Walker Von Schilgen, provided me with invaluable background to their father's carefully handwritten photo captions. The more I learned, the more captivated I became.

I shared the Walker photos and journal with Barbara Wells Sarudy, Director of the Maryland Humanities Council, who insisted that I write an article including a few of the photos for an issue of the council's magazine, *Maryland Humanities*. Her excitement at the sight of the photos inspired me; her confidence that the stories they tell would someday become a book kept me motivated.

Without the help of my friends, there would be no book today. Mary Elizabeth Sells Miklochik patiently traveled with me back and forth to Berlin, and her keen artistic vision was indispensable as we sorted through a thousand photos together. Kaye Brooks Bushel is a top-notch attorney who not only keeps me out of trouble but also helped me research facts and type and edit my manuscript. She is an invaluable friend. Robert N. Hockaday Jr., Bruce Carlin, and

Patrick S. O'Neill encouraged me every step along the way. Robert J. Brugger's enthusiasm for the project has made my experience with the Johns Hopkins University Press most positive. I am grateful to each of them.

My final and dearest expressions of gratitude are to those who have loved, guided, and encouraged me throughout my journey in this world: my late father, Clarence John Sullivan, my dear mother, Sara Robinson Sullivan, and my late wife, Barbara. My precious son, C. John Sullivan III, his wife, Mary Cairnes Sullivan, and my grandson, Benjamin Blair Sullivan, are the ones who make me so intensely aware of the importance of our history, and they are the reasons I am so driven to preserve the past for all of those sure to follow.

Chronology

1868   Stephen Taber, a wealthy Long Islander, obtains a patent from the state of Maryland for a large tract on Assateague Island to use for gunning. He also purchases tracts to the north and south of the patented land.

A group of businessmen form the Atlantic Hotel Company Corporation for the purpose of establishing a seaside resort.

1869   Isaac Coffin builds the first beachfront guest cottage, the Rhode Island Inn, just south of what is now Ocean City.

1872   James Massey builds a guest cottage, which later becomes the Seaside Hotel, at the present-day intersection of Baltimore Avenue and Wicomico Street.

Stephen Taber grants the Atlantic Hotel Company Corporation a 10-acre hotel site across from the narrowest part of the Sinepuxtent Bay and promises to expand the site to 50 acres for a town once the hotel is built.

1874   The Wicomico and Pocomoke Railroad extends to the mainland side of the Sinepuxtent Bay.

Construction begins on the Atlantic Hotel on the oceanfront at Somerset Street.

1875   The stockholders of the Atlantic Hotel Company Corporation meet in Salisbury and name the town "Ocean City."

On July 4, the 400-room Atlantic Hotel opens.

A plat dated August 31, 1875, subdivides the 50-acre parcel into 205 building lots and names the east-west streets, beginning with South Division Street on the southern boundary and ending with Caroline Street on the northern boundary. The north-south avenues are named Atlantic (the Boardwalk), Baltimore, Philadelphia, and St. Louis.

1876   The railroad track extends across the Sinepuxent Bay on a trestle-type bridge, enters Ocean City at South Division Street, and turns up Baltimore Avenue to a depot in front of the Seaside Hotel at Wicomico Street.

1878   The Ocean City Life Saving Station opens at Caroline Street, the northern boundary of the village.

St. Mary's Star of the Sea Catholic Church becomes Ocean City's first church.

1890   The Sinepuxent Beach Company of Baltimore acquires the Atlantic Hotel and 1,600 acres on both sides of the original Ocean City and plats a subdivision bounded on the south by South Tenth Street and on the north by Thirty-third Street.

The Baltimore and Eastern Shore railroad begins operating two trains a day to and from Ocean City.

1892   In August, William G. Walker and Nannie Letitia Wheat are married in Washington, D.C., and honeymoon in Ocean City.

1893   The first coal-burning locomotive enters Ocean City.

1895   The Baltimore, Chesapeake & Atlantic Railway Company opens a ferry line between Baltimore and Claiborne, Maryland, which is served by the steamer *Cambridge*. From Claiborne, the Ocean City Express takes passengers to Ocean City twice daily.

1897   Ocean City's Boardwalk, portions of which were laid in the 1880s, extends to Eighth Street.

1898   St. Rose's Summer Home for Orphans, which later will become the Dominican College, opens on the beach at Fourteenth Street and Atlantic Avenue (the Boardwalk).

1900   The Mt. Pleasant Hotel, located on the Boardwalk between North Division and First Streets, opens.

1901   The Hamilton Hotel opens on the Boardwalk at Third Street.

1903   The railroad depot moves from Baltimore Avenue to Philadelphia Avenue and Somerset Street to alleviate congestion along Ocean City's main street.

1904   William G. Walker and his family vacation at the Mt. Pleasant Hotel in August.

1905   William Walker and his son, Robert, go on their first hunting trip together in Ocean City.

1906   The Ocean City pier opens, featuring a bowling alley, billiard tables, a silent movie theater, refreshment booths, and a dance pavilion.

1908   William Walker purchases Lot 12, Block 20, located at the corner of Baltimore Avenue and Seventh Street, from the Sinepuxent Beach Company.

1909   William Walker builds a hunting lodge on Lot 12.

1910   William Walker builds Romarletta Cottage on the corner of Baltimore Avenue and Seventh Street.

1911   The Dominican Fathers of Catholic University purchase St. Rose's Summer Home for Orphans as a summer home for students preparing for the priesthood. It becomes the Dominican College.

1913   The sand street along Baltimore Avenue to
        N. Third Street is paved during April and May.

1914   Concrete sidewalks improve Baltimore Avenue.

1919   Robert Walker and Dorothy vander Veer are mar-
        ried on June 10, 1919, in Washington, D.C.

1921   William G. Walker, widower, deeds Romarletta to
        his three children but retains the right to occupy
        two furnished rooms in the cottage for life.

1950   The Walkers sell Romarletta.

OLD OCEAN CITY

NANNIE AND ROBERT ON THE RAILROAD
BRIDGE, AUGUST 1903

The Trip

─────

ETWEEN 1876 and 1916, a railroad trestle bridge served as the only bridge over the Sinepuxent Bay connecting Ocean City to the mainland. The bridge design also accommodated one-way pedestrian and wagon traffic. The Walkers and many other early vacationers reached Ocean City by train after a much more complicated trip than today's drive on US 50. Washingtonians took a train to Baltimore and then embarked on a bay steamer headed for Claiborne, a small town across the bay which was the terminus for rail service to Ocean City. On their 1912 trip, the Walkers left Washington on the "12 o'clock express," headed for the B&O's Camden Station in Baltimore. Young Robert, aged eighteen, described the remainder of the trip:

1

June, 18, 1912 Tuesday

After waiting about an hour in Camden station
I walked down to Light Street and boarded the boat
for Claiborne. I stayed in my stateroom and read until
about five o'clock and then had dinner on the steamer.
We reached Claiborne at 5:55 P.M. and took the
"Ocean City Special," on the BC&A [Baltimore, Chesapeake & Annapolis] Railroad. Arrived in Ocean City
at 8:30. Walked up the Boardwalk to Cottage and
opened it up. Bed by 10 P.M.

"Left 706-A St. S.E. Wash. D.C. at 5:45 A.M. via 8th cars to 8th and H. N.E. Electric line to Annapolis, Md. after change of cars at Annapolis Junction. Transfer steamer 'Texas' across Chesapeake Bay to Claiborne and then by rail via BC&A across the 'Eastern Shore,' arriving in Ocean City, Md. at 1:30 P.M."

Left
STEAMSHIPS DOCKED AT
CLAIBORNE HARBOR

Although this description of the Walkers' trip is matter-of-fact, rail travelers of the era experienced many discomforts. There was no air conditioning, and the noisy train showered the passengers with cinders. Indeed, rail travelers often referred to the Baltimore, Chesapeake & Annapolis line as "Bugs, Cinders, and Ashes." Perhaps the social courtesies of the day outweighed the potential discomforts—in 1914, the family reached Claiborne twenty minutes late, "but BC&A train waited for us to dock and hurry aboard."

ROBERT'S FIRST VIEW OF OCEAN CITY
FROM THE TRAIN JUNE 10, 1915

The two-hour steamboat portion of the trip was by far the more pleasant. Bay steamers, such as the *Cambridge*, which transported the Walkers across the Bay in 1913, featured comfortably furnished, first-class staterooms. Silver flatware adorned the tables in the steamers' dining rooms.

By 1915, the Walkers were taking the electric line of the Washington, Baltimore & Annapolis Railway to Annapolis, Maryland, and boarding the steam yacht *Texas* to Claiborne. After arriving at the Ocean City train station, which after 1903 was located at the corner of Philadelphia Avenue and Somerset Street, the family walked to their cottage at Baltimore Avenue and Seventh Street.

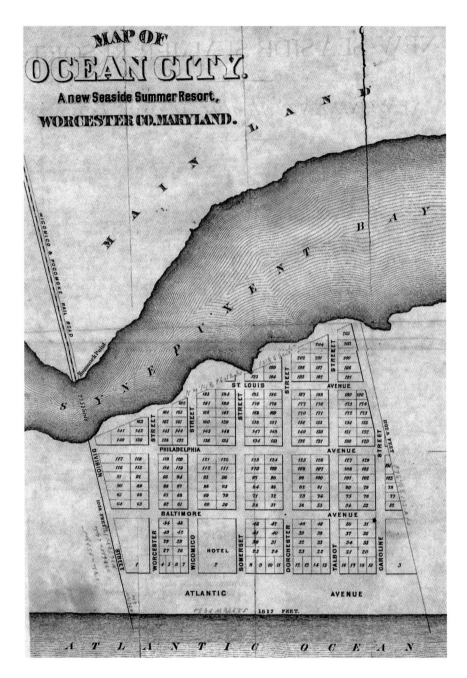

5

ROMARLETTA IN 1914

THE COTTAGE

ROMARLETTA served as the Walkers' summer home for many years. The house incorporated the Walker "hunting lodge"—the structure originally built on the land for the storage of decoys. This lodge became a rear appendage to the house and can still be seen today.

The Walkers' summer sojourns generally lasted from mid-June to mid-September. Opening up the cottage and performing the necessary home repairs usually occupied the first several days of each vacation, but the Walkers found time for target practice right from the start.

June 22, 1912

Spent the morning around the house, carpentering,

painting, etc. Target practice with .22 cal. rifle, off the

boardwalk, with Alex Yearley Jr. all afternoon.

THE WALKERS BUILT THIS HUNTING
LODGE IN AUGUST 1909.
ROBERT, AGED FIFTEEN YEARS,
STANDS IN THE DOOR.
THE HUNTING LODGE BECAME
A PART OF ROMARLETTA THE
FOLLOWING YEAR.

Home improvements, such as building a back porch or a flight of steps from the house up to the front boardwalk, necessitated trips to Berlin, across the Sinepuxent Bay by train, to purchase the lumber. In 1913 Baltimore Avenue was paved to N. Third Street, and by the next year, a new concrete walk had replaced the boardwalk along Baltimore Avenue. The lots immediately surrounding the Walker cottage remained undeveloped.

The family took their meals for the first few days of each summer at the Hamilton Hotel at Third Street and Atlantic Avenue (the Boardwalk). Robert wrote in his journal in June 1912: "I reached home in time to

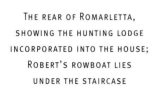

THE REAR OF ROMARLETTA,
SHOWING THE HUNTING LODGE
INCORPORATED INTO THE HOUSE;
ROBERT'S ROWBOAT LIES
UNDER THE STAIRCASE

dress for dinner at the 'Hamilton,' where we are taking our meals until we get a servant." The Hamilton was known for its fine food, but the family also enjoyed dining at the Mt. Pleasant Hotel, which was built in 1900 on the Boardwalk between North Division and First Streets.

Local domestics provided help in setting up house-keeping. On June 16, 1914, the Walkers engaged a Mrs. Moore to help clean Romarletta for the season. She arrived at 7:15 A.M. and began cleaning on the second floor. At 5:30 P.M., she received her day's wage of $1.00 and went home.

VIEW FROM THE FRONT PORCH OF
ROMARLETTA LOOKING EAST,
AUGUST 10, 1912

THE BOARDWALK BETWEEN SEVENTH
AND EIGHTH STREETS, AS SEEN FROM
BALTIMORE AVENUE, CIRCA 1914

ROMARLETTA, *CENTER*, FROM THE
DIRECTION OF THE BOARDWALK. THE LARGE
BUILDING ON THE LEFT, THE LIBERTY FARMS
HOTEL, WAS COMPLETED IN 1925.

"Mt Pleasant Hotel, Ocean City,
Maryland. Shore birds on toast for
supper. They were fine, and Father
promised to give me a gun for
my 10th birthday."

THE MT. PLEASANT STOOD ON THE
BOARDWALK BETWEEN NORTH
DIVISION AND FIRST STREETS

DRESSED FOR DINNER; THE HAMILTON
HOTEL, AUGUST 1905

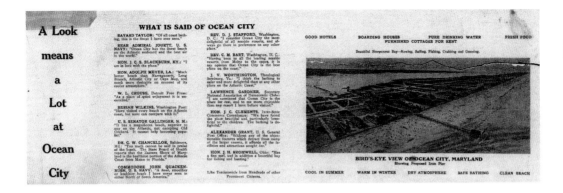

JUNE 20, 1912

"I reached home in time to dress
for dinner at the 'Hamilton' where
we are taking our meals until we
get a servant."

ROBERT AND LETITIA ON
THE BEACH, 1907

THE BEACH

OCEAN CITY's early-twentieth-century vacationers did not spend hours sunbathing, but they enjoyed the beach much as we do today. They fished in the surf, took long walks, hunted for treasure on the beach, rode ponies, and swam.

June 25, 1912 Tuesday

Rain. Spent most of morning talking to Yearleys and Booths. Fishing along surf for about a half-hour in afternoon. Caught nothing as a strong southeast wind caused a drift up the beach and I could not keep my line out. After supper I went down to meet the 8:28 train. Howard came down after a day with the dentist.

ROBERT, AGE TEN, IN THE SURF,
AUGUST 1904

ROBERT AND LETITIA ON
THE BEACH, 1905

ROBERT AND LETITIA
IN THE SURF, 1907

LETITIA ON A PONY IN FRONT OF THE HAMILTON HOTEL,
WITH EFFIE HOLDING MARGARET IN THE
BACKGROUND, 1908

They enjoyed long walks on a beach that was devoid of the crowds of today, but they encountered some hazards the modern-day beachcomber does not.

NANNIE AND WILLIAM BY THE SURF,
JUNE 1908

June 30, 1912 Sunday

We then walked up the beach as far as an old iron buoy (about 1/2 mile south of Isle of Wight L.S.S. [life-saving station]) about 4 miles from home. . . . A skeleton of a horse is stranded on the main spit at Reedy Point [Fifty-fourth Street], but the buzzards are not leaving much on it to bother us.

AUNT HATTIE DUNNINGTON WITH
LETITIA AND ROBERT ON
THE BEACH, 1909

ᴀᴜɴᴛ Hᴀᴛᴛɪᴇ ᴏɴ ᴛʜᴇ ʙᴇᴀᴄʜ ɪɴ ꜰʀᴏɴᴛ
ᴏꜰ ᴛʜᴇ Yᴇᴀʀʟᴇʏ ᴄᴏᴛᴛᴀɢᴇ

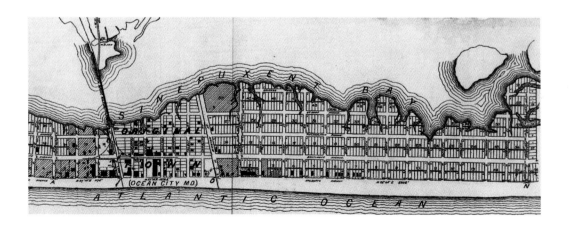

LETITIA AND MARGARET HAVING A TEA
PARTY BY THE DUNES, 1911

July 7, 1912 Sunday

Took a walk up the beach with Howard in afternoon.
Neither of us wore socks with our "sneakers" and we
plowed through "poison ivy" and "poison oak" several
times. I don't think that they affect me much but I am
afraid Howard will have his troubles.

Robert collected "treasures" on his walks on the beach. Sometimes these treasures were shells—sea turtle, king crab, and conch—but he also collected old coins, presumably deposited in the ocean by shipwrecks that had washed up on the beach. Robert placed these coins in a carefully labeled box, which is still intact.

Shipwrecks provided additional entertainment for these vacationers. On March 13, 1912, the three-masted lumber schooner *John W. Hall* ran aground about two and a half miles south of the Ocean City Life Saving Station. The wreck became a place for hunting, fishing, and climbing.

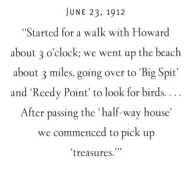

JUNE 23, 1912
"Started for a walk with Howard
about 3 o'clock; we went up the beach
about 3 miles, going over to 'Big Spit'
and 'Reedy Point' to look for birds. . . .
After passing the 'half-way house'
we commenced to pick up
'treasures.'"

ROBERT LEADING LETITIA ON A PONY
ALONG THE BEACH

A SWIM IN THE BAY, 1913

THE *JOHN W. HALL* WAS USED AS
A PLATFORM FOR DIVING AND SHORE
BIRD SHOOTING DURING THE SUMMERS
OF 1912 AND 1913

July 17, 1912 Wednesday

Spent the morning at home. Bath in surf at 12. Coldest water ever. In about 20 minutes. About 3 o'clock started down to the wreck with Howard. He carried a fishing line and I my Automatic gun with full choke barrel, decoys and 15 shells. We sat on the wreck from 4 P.M. until about 5:30 and didn't see a bird. Howard caught 2 small king fish by dropping his line over the bow of the boat. He used "ole wives," a small fish, for bait.

24

> Sept 6 [1913] Saturday

Left Jarvis' wharf at 4 P.M. with Mrs. Newman, Pierce, Artemesa, Martha and Helen Newman, Julia Nicol and the dog for a sail down to see the wreck at the Inlet. . . . We walked over to the wreck and found plenty of birds. Martha shot four times with my gun, killing 2 sandpipers. Pierce shot once killing four out of a flock of six sitting on the beach and Miss Nicol shot once without killing anything. . . . Martha tried to climb up on the wreck but slipped on the old moss covered deck and slid almost into the water.

Robert Walker swam at least once a day, weather permitting, and referred to his daily swims as "bathes." Occasionally, he recorded the length of his swim by landmarks.

> Aug. 4 [1915]

Swim at noon from Hamilton Hotel to Haimar.

DOROTHY AND ROBERT BESIDE
THE BOARDWALK, 1919

DOROTHY VAN DER VEER BY
THE SURF, 1916

Aug. 5 [1915]

Swim from "Breakers" [Third Street] to North 7th St.
(with tide).

DOMINICAN BROTHERS AND MARGARET
ON THE PORCH OF THE COLLEGE

THE DOMINICAN BROTHERS

AMONG the early-twentieth-century summer residents in Ocean City were the Dominican brothers who came to stay at the retreat known as the Dominican College, located on the beach between Thirteenth and Fourteenth Streets. The Walkers were devout Catholics and enjoyed the friendship of these summer residents. Young Robert Walker reported spending many hours with the brothers and novices at target practice, playing checkers, bathing in the ocean, shooting shore birds, and boating. Their days together started early, ended late, and included repair projects on the college property.

July 26, 1912 Friday

Played checkers in the forenoon with the novices at
the Dominican College. . . . Went to Berlin with the
"Brothers" to watch a ball game between the Dominican Brothers team and the Berlin team. Final score 11
to 10 in favor of the Brothers.

Top

THE DOMINICAN COLLEGE, WHICH STOOD
UP THE BEACH BETWEEN THIRTEENTH AND
FOURTEENTH STREETS, 1912. A PORTION OF
THE STRUCTURE STILL STANDS AND IS USED
AS A DORMITORY FOR EMPLOYEES OF
PHILLIPS RESTAURANT

Bottom

THE DOMINICAN COLLEGE
IN SEPTEMBER 1915

Two of Robert's shooting companions
standing in front of Romarletta

The Dominican College after the
storm of 1918, with sand piled
high in front of the steps

ONE OF THE DOMINICAN FATHERS
MOTORING ON THE NEWLY PAVED
BALTIMORE AVENUE, 1915

July 31 [1913] Thursday. My 19th Birthday

Up at 4:15 and started up the beach at 4:30. Stopped at the Dominican College for Brother Matthew and at 5 o'clock we walked up to a blind on the surfbank just abreast of "Big Spit" and set out 2 dozen decoys. We had fair luck on beach and later tried Big Spit but there were no birds traveling the bay. Home at 9:30 with 20 grey backs, 1 killdeer and 1 "calico back" or ruddy turnstone of which I killed all but 6 of the grey backs with 16 shells. . . . Bath with the Brothers at 11 o'clock. Spent the afternoon carpentering with Brother

"Allie." After late supper I worked with "Reg" on the cement engine pier in the tower until 11 o'clock.

The tower Robert and Brother Reg worked on was the lighthouse-like structure that housed the water system for the Dominican College. It no longer stands, but part of the college, which operated as the Broadripple Hotel for many years, remains.

DOROTHY AND ROBERT LEAVING FOR CHURCH, AUGUST 1919

SHOOTING FROM A BLIND ON THE
SINEPUXENT BAY; THE RAILROAD BRIDGE
APPEARS IN THE DISTANCE

Days Filled with Sport

THE WALKERS' annual pilgrimage to the ocean included many days filled with traditional Maryland sports, especially shooting. They shot targets, both fixed and flying. For practice they threw clay targets over the ocean, the marsh, and nearby open fields. Robert and his mother engaged in target practice from the side porch of Romarletta. They shot wildfowl over the beach and the marsh. During the months of Robert Walker's vacation, migrating shore birds were in season. Shore bird shooting along the Atlantic seaboard was one of the most popular sports of the nineteenth and early twentieth centuries. Both sportsmen and commercial market hunters harvested millions of these

JULY 14, 1912

"In afternoon I walked up to Big Spit
with a half dozen decoys to try and
get some photographs of birds. Had
no success as high tide in the bay
completely flooded all the spits"

birds. Market hunters sold their kills to markets in the

big cities. Sport hunters shot for the mere sport of it,

to test their skills against nature's and to feast on the

delicious fowl with family and friends. Fine restau-

rants served local shore birds as delicacies. In August

of 1903, nine-year-old Robert Walker dined on "shore

birds on toast" with his father at the Mt. Pleasant

Hotel.

A successful outing usually required the use of decoys. On the beach, the shore bird hunter placed the decoys at the surf's edge and dug a sand pit as a blind. When natural materials such as driftwood or grasses were available on the beach, the shooter further disguised himself. The marsh hunter placed his decoys in shallow water and built his blind of grasses and brush.

AUGUST 15, 1913

"Just at supper time I saw a large heron feeding in the slough back of our cottage and after supper I crawled back on it and when it flew at about 30 yds. range I broke its wing by a shot from the right barrel of my Fox double gun using a shell loaded 3-Deadshot 1 1/8 # 8c. It was a Great Blue Heron having a wing spread of exactly six feet and a length from bill to feet extended of five feet."

A BAREFOOT ROBERT PROUDLY POSING WITH HIS GUN AND "KILL" IN FRONT OF THE COTTAGE

Decoys are a unique accessory of North American waterfowl shooting. They have been used more extensively on the Atlantic coast of North America than anywhere in the world. The use of decoys can be traced back to the Native Americans, who used natural bird skins or birds formed of marsh grasses as decoys. Mimicking the Native Americans, the earliest settlers formed shore bird likenesses of wood.

THE WALKERS' CHESAPEAKE BAY RETRIEVER, BROWNIE, IN THE SINEPUXENT

"JUST ME" [ROBERT] AND A CORNER OF POWELL'S HOUSEBOAT, DEC. 29, 1916; TINGLES' ISLAND, MARYLAND

Typically, local carvers created these decoys from pine or cedar. Some were merely "flatties," or silhouettes, while others were full bodied and painstakingly carved with great detail. The early decoy makers did not have patterns to follow, so they used freshly killed specimens of each species as patterns taken from

nature. While sport shooters and market hunters in-itially created their own decoys, entrepreneurs quickly recognized the tremendous demand and began to produce decoys in factories as well. Several factories manufactured shore bird decoys in great quantities before 1890. These creations were both practical and beautiful.

William and Robert Walker carved both flatties and full-bodied decoys for their rig. Photographs taken by the Walkers of their decoy rig show a variety of flatties, factory decoys, and hand-carved full bodies. Young Robert also created flat sheet-tin or iron decoys, carrying on patterns initially created by his father.

REEDY POINT AT OCEAN CITY, MARYLAND,
SEPTEMBER 1916

ROBERT WALKER, *RIGHT*, AND SHOOTING
COMPANION, MOSQUITO VEILS IN PLACE,
WITH HANDS FULL OF SHORE BIRDS

Sometimes nature provided the decoys. Robert reported using oyster and clam shells along with his decoys, which when positioned upright in the sand, mimicked small shore birds. In his journal Robert included detailed descriptions of how to make and paint shore bird decoys of all species native to the Ocean City surf.

SHORE BIRD DECOYS

Willet 16 in. from tip of bill to tip of tail

Curlew 23 in. from tip of bill to tip of tail

Greater Yellow Leg 13 in. from tip of bill to
    tip of tail

Lesser Yellow Leg 11 in. from tip of bill to tip of tail

Jack Snipe 9 in. from tip of bill to tip of tail

Robin Snipe 10 1/2 in. from tip of bill to tip of tail

For coloring lay on 2 coats of thick white lead all over as a ground coloring. To make a yellow leg of him speckle the neck and breast with dark slate spots, paint the head and back slate gray, spot with little white-gray herringbones, leave the rump white, also underbody, bar the tail with gray cross-stripes, outline the

MAY 1917

"*Black breasted Plover* killed at fifty yards range on the beach north of O.C., Maryland; single shot off hand from Colt .32 cal. Long Pocket *Positive Revolver* by R. C. Walker"

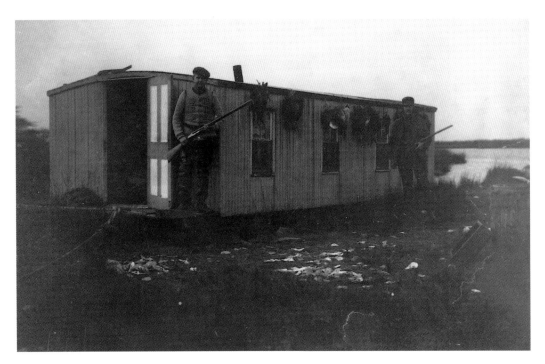

"Joshua T. Bowden, Ocean City, Md. Black ducks and stray Redheads & Geese. Hunt from point blinds, living in house boat on marsh 2 mi north of Ocean City. No regular rates charged but he would be glad to feed you and furnish rig of live decoys for $2.50 per day."

wings, adding heavy black edgings towards the tips, give him a black bill and a yellow 3/8 in. dowel 15 in. long for a leg.

To make a jack snipe of him edge the herringbones on his back with rusty red, lay a thin wash of olive over the gray and white markings on his wings, and give him a brown stick for a leg. Be sure and put plenty of turpentine in the paint to kill the luster of the oil as the flash of sunlight on glossy decoys is fatal.

(The 10 in. size decoy will answer for jack snipe, lesser yellow legs, robin snipe, dowitchers, knots, etc.)

To paint a robin snipe proceed as before but make the breast, neck and head a rich yellowish brown, wing covered whitish gray speckled with slate gray dots; back chocolate brown with black herringbone markings, tail white barred with dark slate.

The measurements given are overall. Allowing 1 1/2 inches for bill, the balance is the length of the body of the bird.

Bend a piece of soft wire to form a natural outline of the bird with leg out for decoys from this as a pattern.

Plover decoys should be 10 to 11 1/2 in. Head and neck white, breast black and rest brown.

Made 6 flat decoys and 6 good round body Robin Snipe decoys during winter and spring of 1911–1912. During 1912 season I had from 20 to 24 decoys counting some I found at different times along the beach. About 12 of these were fairly good decoys.

FRANK STANDING IN HIS BOAT WITH
A LIVE DECOY CAGE AT HIS FEET,
SEPTEMBER 1934

The Walkers—sometimes with members of the Dominican community—did not confine their shore bird hunting to Ocean City proper. They often traveled by boat south to Tingles Island and north to the Isle of Wight Bay and present-day Fenwick in pursuit of game. They hunted at Reedy Point, Grassey Island, Sandy Point, Big Spit, Dog and Bitch Islands, Alecks Pines, and Zippies Creek, some of which remain, while others have disappeared.

August 26 [1913] Tuesday Clear with southeast breeze. Up at 1 a.m. Met Brothers Gabriel, Jerome, Matthew, Thomas and Reginald on boardwalk at 1:30 and we reached Bill Powell's launch, anchored below the railroad bridge, at 2 o'-clock but a faulty spark gap adjustment delayed us about 30 minutes. We reached Tingles Island at dawn, Powell running the boat in almost to the site of the old Sturgeon Shanty. Then we poled up Sturgeon slough, which leads to the north end of the big levels. The levels and east ponds were dry so we shot on the west side

ROBERT PLACING BLACKDUCK
DECOYS IN THE BAY MARSH

of the levels in the chain of small ponds on the marsh. Mosquitoes were <u>fierce</u>! We walked south about 3/4 mile through the marsh and then Tom & I put out decoys in the northern most pond and waited for the birds. The water was 6 inches deep in the blind but we had each brought an empty shotgun shell box so we managed to keep fairly dry. I whistled one flock of about a dozen down to the decoys and killed 5 in two shots while Tom shot both barrels to get three. The rest of the shooting was at singles and doubles as what few flocks we saw, would not decoy. We shot until 2 P.M. and then returned to the boat with 150 yellowlegs for the crowd. I killed 54 yellowlegs and 1 robin snipe with 113 shells used. I made several shots at long range only wounding my birds and then had to use the other barrel to bring them down. Nearly all of the rest of my misses resulted from shooting at single birds after they had swung into line with the sun. Once a pair came in and I waited for them to cross and then killed both at one shot. Tom killed 10 yellowlegs with about 12 shots, Jerome got 31 with 59 shells, Gabriel 12 with 30 shells, Matt 31 with 38 shells. Reginald killed 10 with 29 shells and Bill Powell shot a dozen times with a double gun "strange to him" and only killed one yellowleg. Home at 5:30 P.M. Bath in the surf after supper and bed by 8 P.M.

Robert frequently reported in his journal the number of shells required to kill a specified number of birds and compared his prowess with that of the other members of his shooting party. The spirit of competition was very much alive in these excursions. Robert was also very protective of his territory when shooting.

September 3, 1912 Tuesday

Went hunting up the beach by myself after dinner. Walked to the first blind a very deep one just above the Big Sand dune and put out 6 wooden decoys and about 10 oysters shells. Mr. Buell and his boy Arthur came up about 4 o'clock and claimed the blind I was in on the ground that they had dug it. I told them that possession was 9/10 of the law and they walked up the beach and dug another.

July 21, 1913

Walked about one mile above north end of boardwalk and built a blind of driftwood on the crest of the surf bank. . . . A half hour later two hunters came up the beach and stopped to ask for the loan of some decoys but as they intended to build another blind just north of me and in the direction from which the birds were coming, I refused them.

Robert, nevertheless, happily shared his knowledge of the sport. On August 9, 1912, he wrote: "Met Paul Malone, a boy about 14, just learning to shoot, and gave him a few tips as to location and size of blind, setting out decoys and proper shooting range."

Crows and doves were also fair game for Ocean City sportsmen. These were usually hunted on the farms across the Sinepuxent Bay.

July 30 [1915]

Rowed out to the island (southernmost) back of the Brothers with [Brother] Jerry to shoot crows but did not get a shot between 5 and 6 A.M. After Breakfast we sailed across the bay in my boat to shoot crows on the farms from Johnson's to Garrett's. We only killed one but we obtained permission from both Dave Johnson and W. E. Garrett to shoot doves after August 15 on their wheat fields.

DOROTHY, DRESSED IN A SAILOR SUIT
AND READY TO HUNT ON
THE BEACH, 1916

SPORTSWOMEN

ESPITE the appearance of delicate femininity suggested by the long dresses, large hats, and parasols of the day, many women who vacationed in Ocean City at the turn of the century hunted shore birds with the same enthusiasm as their male counterparts. Robert recorded many hunting trips with female companions during his Ocean City summers. The location of these activities is surprising: they often hunted on the beach. In August 1912 Robert wrote of engaging in target practice with his mother off the side porch of their cottage at Baltimore Avenue and Seventh Street!

Robert's descriptions of hunting expeditions with various female vacationers reveal that they participated on equal footing with their companions.

LETITIA WALKER AFTER A PRACTICE
SHOT WITH HER MOTHER'S PARKER
20GA SHOTGUN, 1914

AUGUST 22, 1916

"She knelt up to aim and the bird flew but she swung the gun up over it with the proper lead and killed her first bird flying like a true sportswoman and an expert. After the first shock, she responded to the fascination of the sport and wanted to try again on another."

August 19, 1912 Monday

Called for Mrs. Kearney at 2 P.M. and we started up the beach. . . . I showed Mrs. Kearney how to find Big Spit and how to arrange her decoys. I shot twice, once at a pair of bullhead plover out of range and once at a ring neck plover over on Big Spit which I killed. Mrs. Kearney killed 2 grey backs as they pitched singly to the decoys. We hurried home to avoid a storm from the north west but were caught just above the Big Sand dune. We both were wet to the skin when we reached home about 6 o'clock.

DOROTHY AND LETITIA ON THE BAY
AFTER A MORNING SHOOT, 1919

Invariably, the days spent hunting with female companions appear to have been crammed with a variety
of activities, but the Walkers also found time for relig-
ious obligations.

August 30 [1913] Saturday

Started for Mr. Newman's blind in his sailboat at 9:30
A.M. with Pierce, his father, Miss Newman, Miss Mar-

tha Newman, and Julia Nicols of Manassas, Va. . . .
By five o'clock I had killed exactly a dozen grey backs
with 18 shells. Miss Newman shot once with my gun
at three little grey backs on the beach but missed. We
had a picnic lunch in the blind and at 5 o'clock returned to the boat. On the way home each of the
younger girls shot my gun once and Miss Newman
shot her father's autoloading Winchester three times
using my shells and was promised a 20 ga gun as a re-
ward for her "bravery." We reached the wharf at 7 P.M.
and after stopping at the church for confession we
went in the ocean. That is Mr. Newman, Martha and
Miss Newman and I did and it was fine but very dark
and rough. Home by 8:30 P.M. Bed by 10:30 P.M. Total
25 shells.

In August 1916 Robert made an entry in his journal
about teaching a young woman about his own age to
hunt shore birds.

54

Sailed up to Big Spit with Dorothy at three P.M. . . .
Later a single plover pitched outside the decoys about
thirty yards away and I handed Dorothy my gun with
instructions to shoot it. She knelt up to aim and the
bird flew but she swung the gun up over it with the
proper lead and killed her first bird flying like a true
sportswoman and an expert. After the first shock, she
responded to the fascination of the sport and wanted
to try again on another.

That young woman was Dorothy van der Veer of
Somerville, New Jersey, a distant cousin of Robert's
who was visiting Ocean City with her family that
summer. Dorothy's hunting interest rivaled Robert's
and his family's, and on June 10, 1919, Dorothy and
Robert were married in Washington, D.C.

Robert's mother and sisters also engaged in the sport
of hunting shore birds. Photographs of the female
family members at target practice or posed with their
weapons fill the photograph albums.

Top right
DOROTHY, WITH HER SHOOTING
COACH, TAKES A PRACTICE SHOT AT A
CLAY TARGET, OCTOBER 1934

Bottom right
DOROTHY AND HER PARKER
20GA IN A BAY-SIDE BLIND,
OCTOBER 1934

DOROTHY SEATED IN THE STERN
OF ONE OF ROBERT'S BOATS
IN HER BATHING SUIT

Boating

────────

T HE WALKERS also enjoyed boating
during their summer vacations. In mid-
July 1912, Robert wrote in his journal of
his pleasure upon receiving the Knock-
Down Motor Boat he had ordered from the Brooks
Manufacturing Company of Saginaw, Michigan. He
also recorded many sailing trips that he made by himself and with companions. While the boat often provided transportation to a desired hunting spot, boat
trips were mostly for the pleasure of the trip and a picnic lunch.

On occasion, Robert and his companions rented a
boat for fishing and got more than they bargained for.

OUT FOR A SAIL: MARGARET, NANNIE,
AUNT HATTIE, AND ROBERT

August 23, 1912

Went down to Jarvis Wharf and to L.S.S. to see about
hiring Joe Quillen's powerboat for a hunt down the
bay on Saturday.

Left home at 8 A.M. for all day hunting trip down the bay. Met Brother Jerome (Tracey) on the boardwalk and we started down to the wharf to get the boat ready. We rowed out to the stake and tried to start the engine but it wouldn't start. We rowed in to Buntings' Wharf and Harry Bunting and a couple of other "marine engineers" monkeyed with the engine. I discovered a leak in the compression inlet pipe and stopped it with 2 turns of adhesive plaster. Finally started about 10 o'clock.

A BUSINESS CARD FOUND AMONG ROBERT WALKER'S OCEAN CITY MEMORABILIA

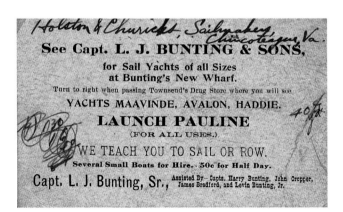

AUGUST 22, 1916

"Sailed up to Big Spit with Dorothy
at three P.M. Killed 1 winter yellowleg
from Boat on way up and 'went about'
to pick it up."

Robert's journal reveals how much Ocean City and
the adjoining mainland have changed in the interven-
ing years. In July of 1915, Robert, his parents, his Aunt
Hattie, and his two sisters sailed to the Isle of Wight.

Started at 2 P.M. for picnic to Isle of Wight with
Father, Mother, Hattie, Letitia & Margaret in my sailboat. Almost a dead calm but light northeast breeze
enabled us to reach the old Indian Landing on the
northeastern shore of the Island by 4 P.M. Toured
island, noticing trenches dug for "buried treasure" and
site for boring for an old dry oil well (N.G.), picked
blackberries which were extremely plentiful, and visited the caretaker ("Frank Shockley") at his house.
Picnic supper near Indian Landing at 5 P.M. and started
home at 6:15. Light southeast breeze but by poling
succeeded in reaching home by 8 P.M.

Aug 5 [1915]

Started for the deep slough just north of Big Spit at 4
P.M. with Aunt Hattie, Mother, Margaret, "Jerry" in
my sailboat. Brisk southeast breeze enabled us to sail
straight up past Big Spit and then we took down the
sail and poled up almost to the line of sand dunes in a
deep and narrow slough. Walked over to the beach by
4:45 and waited until 5:30 for Father, Aunt Annie,

Dorothy in her sailor suit,
August 1916

Letitia and the servant who walked up the beach. We
returned to my boat for a picnic supper at 6 o'clock
and then as a northwest cloudbank threatened rain
and a "blow" we started for home at 7 p.m. I took Annie, Hattie, Letitia, "Jerry" and the "maid" with me in
the boat while the rest walked. Aunt Annie and the
servant were both very much frightened by the big

waves out on the bay and Annie kept insisting that I head straight for Ocean City instead of zig-zagging all over the bay (tacking into a strong head wind). However, I refused to stop to let them off and finally reached my wharf in safety at a quarter to eight.

Dorothy in Robert's sailboat on a calm Sinepuxent Bay

THE *JOHN W. HALL* WAS GROUNDED ABOUT 2-1/2 MILES
SOUTH OF THE OCEAN CITY LIFE SAVING STATION,
MARCH 1912

THE DANGERS OF THE OCEAN

———

WHILE the Walkers and their fellow vacationers came to enjoy the pleasures of the seashore, on occasion they were reminded of the ocean's force. In June of 1912, Robert walked down the beach with a friend to photograph the wreck of the *John W. Hall*. Robert reported in his journal:

The 3 masted lumber schooner John W. Hall of Frederica, Delaware shifted cargo and leaking badly was finally grounded about 2 1/2 miles south of O.C.L.S.S. and directly south of the site of the old "Inlet" [nature had reclosed this opening in the barrier island five years earlier] on the morning of March 13, 1912. The crew were saved by the O.C. L. S. crew by means of the "breeches-buoy." A severe "northeaster" drove the wreck up high and dry on the point. Dynamite was used by the salvage company in releasing the cargo and most of the deck was blown off. No signs of birds.

The ocean was a challenge to property owners on land as well. On August 31, 1913, Robert wrote of the high tide that evening:

Home by 7:15 and found an extremely high tide with water running completely around the house and through the cellar. Worked about 20 minutes shoveling sand around my engine to keep it dry and then spent the rest of the evening until half past ten in writing up this diary.

Ocean City pier wrecked by the weight
of snow and ice from the storm of
January 20–23, 1914

The Isle of Wight life-saving
station, 1914

THE FENWICK LIGHTHOUSE ON
THE MARYLAND-DELAWARE
LINE, 1919

Below

THE BOARDWALK UNDER SIEGE BY
THE OCEAN; THE TOWER PICTURED
SITS IN FRONT OF THE U.S.
COAST GUARD STATION

OCEAN CITY LIFEGUARDS
AT PRACTICE, 1919

Far more dramatic is Robert's report of an accident in the early morning hours of July 1, 1915:

Fatal fish-boat accident on the bar just below south end of the boardwalk at 5:30 A.M. A 36 ft. dory (power) with crew of seven men capsized on the bar on way out to the pounds either a stern line fouling the propeller wheel or water in the carburetor stopping

STORM WRECKAGE OF THE SCHMITT,
KIMBALL, AND PILLINGS COTTAGES,
FEBRUARY 9, 1920

the engine. No oars, so the next big sea slewed the boat around in the trough of waves and parallel to the beach and then a big wave breaking on the bar, filled the boat and capsized it, throwing all of the crew into a heavy sea, kicked up by a strong southeast gale. It is the off season for the Government Life Savers but one power fishing boat and two small dorys put off to the rescue. Each succeeded in picking up one man and another managed to swim ashore unassisted, but the other three washed out to sea and one of the rescued was dead by the time he was brought ashore. One body was picked up on the beach about three miles north of the site of the disaster just 24 hours later (at low tide). Another was found at about the same place 48 hours after the wreck occurred and the third had not been washed ashore at the time of this writing.

Several days later Robert wrote of walking along the beach looking for the body of the still missing seaman, Luther Hitchins. He stopped at the Isle of Wight C.G.S. (Coast Guard Station) and Acting Keeper John Wallace [Willis] Hudson served him breakfast.

THE BOARDWALK LOOKING SOUTH FROM
THE HAMILTON HOTEL AT N. THIRD STREET,
AUGUST 1905

AFTER SUPPER

———

The Boardwalk and Other
Amusements

WHILE Ocean City vacationers such as the Walkers engaged in some leisure activities unheard of today, surprisingly similar pursuits filled their after-supper hours. The Boardwalk of that period was much different than it is today, but even then it was a "destination."

The 4th of July 1912 began with an activity no longer permitted in Ocean City but ended as Independence Day typically does.

July 4, 1912 Thursday

Target practice in the morning with Alex Yearley &
Howard. Bath in surf about 12:15. Very cold and
rough. Took a walk up the beach after dinner. Went
up on "Big Spit" and shot at a snipe with 22 cal. rifle.
No signs of birds on the beach. After supper went over
to Booth's to watch fireworks display. Bed by 10.

Downtown Ocean City offered a variety of amusements. Joseph Schaefer operated an establishment at
Baltimore Avenue and Somerset Street, just two blocks

JOSEPH SCHAEFER'S BAKERY AND
DELICATESSEN AT THE CORNER OF
BALTIMORE AVENUE AND SEVENTH STREET;
WHEN THIS PHOTOGRAPH WAS TAKEN
DURING THE SUMMER OF 1913, BALTIMORE
AVENUE WAS BEING PAVED

DURING THE SUMMER OF 1913, THIS
HOUSE, AT THE CORNER OF BALTIMORE
AVENUE AND TALBOT STREET, WAS
OCCUPIED BY THE NEWMAN FAMILY OF
WASHINGTON, D.C.; THE HOUSE LATER
BECAME THE TALBOT INN

from the Newmans' house, which offered baked goods,

delicatessen items, and confections. The Ocean City

pier, constructed prior to 1910, included a dance

pavilion, skating rink, bowling alleys, and poolroom

in addition to the theater.

THE ROLLER SKATING RINK LOCATED
AT THE END OF THE PIER

Sept. 5 [1913] Friday

Downtown in the afternoon and visited the Newmans
in the evening. Played checkers with Pierce [New-
man]. I won two games and the other was a draw.
Then we went to moving pictures on the pier and to
Shafer's for ice cream. Home at 11 P.M.

Right
A RARE SIGHTING ON THE
SINEPUXENT BAY, 1917

In the summer of 1913, the Newman family of Washington, D.C., friends of the Walkers, resided in a large house located at the corner of Baltimore Avenue and Talbot Street. By 1920 the house had become the Talbot Inn.

September 14 [1913] Sunday

Called on the Newmans at 8 P.M. and spent the evening with Martha and Artemesa on the boardwalk and on their porch until 11 P.M.

FRANK IN HIS SOAPBOX, 1921

EPILOGUE

THE WALKERS were one of the millions of families that have vacationed in Ocean City over the last 130 years. For them and many others, Ocean City was a place to return to year after year. Many families kept albums filled with photographs of generations enjoying this wonderful summer place, but the Walker family preserved more than just a record of their family. William and his son, Robert, photographed the development of Ocean City in its early years, including the unique pastimes of that era. They carefully recorded dates, events, and descriptions on the back of those photographs, and Robert recorded additional details of those long-ago summer days in his vacation journal. Their work offers us a lively journey back in time, as strangers in a place we thought we knew.

The Walkers continued to enjoy Ocean City and Romarletta for many years. Nannie Walker died in 1920, and William deeded Romarletta to his three children in 1921, retaining the use of two furnished rooms in the house for his lifetime. Robert and Dorothy lived in Washington, D.C., and in Scarsdale and Bronxville, New York, in the years after their marriage, but they returned to Ocean City with their six children—Frank, Scotty, Ann, Virginia, Katherine, and Donald—for many years. One of their children, Scotty, was born in Ocean City. It was not until 1950, when Letitia and Margaret sold Romarletta, that the Walker family sojourns came to an end.

FRANK RUNNING IN THE SURF

Frank in his pram with a surf rod,
August 1922

Letitia out for a ride,
August 1925

AFTER HUNTING SHORE BIRDS, FRANK
AND SCOTTY RETURN WITH MORE WOODEN
DECOYS THAN BIRDS

AUNT LETITIA HELPS SCOTTY ONTO
THE PONY BEHIND FRANK

FRANK, AGE TEN—WITH COOKIES,
SANDWICH, AND GUN—OUT FOR A DAY'S
SPORT, OCTOBER 1930

ROBERT IN BERMUDA DURING
WORLD WAR II, JULY 1943